Love to Stay
Leader Guide

Also by Adam Hamilton

ADAM HAMILTON

LOVE TO STAY

SEX, GRACE, AND COMMITMENT

LEADER GUIDE
BY JOHN P. GILBERT

Abingdon Press
Nashville

Adam Hamilton

Love to Stay:
Sex, Grace, and Commitment

Leader Guide

ISBN 978-1-4267-5954-3

Scripture quotations, unless marked otherwise, are from the New
Revised Standard Version of the Bible, copyrighted © 1989 by
the Division of Christian Education of the National Council of the
Churches of Christ in the United States of America, and are used by
permission.

Library of Congress Cataloging-in-Publication applied for.

13 14 15 16 17 18 19 20 21 22—10 9 8 7 6 5 4 3 2 1

MANUFACTURED IN THE UNITED STATES OF AMERICA

Contents

TO THE LEADER

Welcome! In this study, you have an exciting opportunity to learn and grow with a group of Christians seeking to understand God's plan for love and marriage.

You'll be leading the group, but always remember that you are also one of the learners. Your job is not to judge answers or grade responses but to facilitate the group's study and to engage in the learning process yourself.

The aim of the study is to explore the topic of marriage and loving relationships. The six-session study is made up of several components:

- Adam Hamilton's book *Love to Stay: Sex, Grace, and Commitment*
- a DVD in which Hamilton, using stories and Scripture, presents key points from the book
- this Leader Guide

Using these components, you will lead the members of your group over the course of six sessions. Encourage everyone in your group to keep a Bible close by during the study and to bring it to each session.

What the Study Is and Is Not

Talking about marriage and love relationships is always interesting and thought provoking. To do so within the context of the Christian faith makes the discussion doubly rewarding. But first, here are some words of caution. The study *is not*:

- a cure-all for troubled marriages,
- a replacement for premarital counseling,
- a recipe book or a tested formula: "Do this, and you'll have a happy marriage."

Here's what the study *is*:

- an exploration of the meaning and mission of marriage, a relationship in which each person blesses the other;
- a careful consideration of data that point to factors making for a happy marriage;
- assurance that, no matter how happy people are in a marriage relationship, difficulties will arise that can be met with confidence, faith, and love.

Does this all mean that the study is only for those who are married? Of course not! We learn from each other, so the married couples will learn from those who are not married, and singles will gain valuable insight from their married friends.

Are you ready to look at marriage relationships in a deep and joyful way? Let's get started!

Session Format

Because no two groups are alike, this guide has been designed to give you flexibility and choice in tailoring the sessions for your group. The session activities are listed below. You may choose any or all, adapting them as you wish to meet the schedule and needs of your particular group.

You may find that your session time is too short to do all the activities; if so, you can select ahead of time which activities the group will do, for how long, and in what order.

Getting Started
    Session Goals
    Opening Prayer
    Biblical Foundation
    Opening Activity

Learning Together
    Video Study and Discussion
    Book Study and Discussion
    Bible Study and Discussion

Wrapping Up
    Closing Activity
    Closing Prayer

Helpful Hints

Preparing for the session
- Become familiar with the material before the group session. Read the book chapter and watch the video segment.
- Choose the session elements you will use during the group session, including the specific discussion questions you plan to cover.
- Secure a TV and DVD player in advance.
- Oversee the room's setup. Ideally, group members should be seated around a table or in a circle so that all can see each other. Moveable chairs are best because the group will be breaking up into small teams.
- Bring a supply of Bibles for those who forget to bring their own. Having a variety of translations is helpful.
- Provide paper and pens or pencils at each session, and encourage group members to bring their own notepads.

• You will also need a chalkboard, a white board, or an easel with paper for each session.

Setting the Tone
• Begin and end on time.
• Be enthusiastic! Create a climate of participation, encouraging group members to participate as they feel comfortable.
• Communicate the importance of group discussions and group exercises.
• If no one answers at first during discussions, do not be afraid of a silence. Count silently to ten; then say something such as, "Would anyone like to go first?" If no one responds, venture an answer yourself and ask for other comments.
• Model openness as you share with the group. Group members will follow your example. If you limit your sharing to a surface level, others will follow suit.
• Encourage multiple answers or responses before moving on.
• Ask, "Why?" or "Why do you believe that?" to help continue a discussion and give it greater depth.
• Affirm others' responses with comments such as "Great" or "Thanks" or "Good insight"—especially if this is the first time someone has spoken during the group session.
• Give everyone a chance to talk, but keep the conversation moving. Moderate to prevent a few individuals from doing all the talking.
• Monitor your own contributions. If you are doing most of the talking, back off so that you do not train the group to listen rather than speak up.
• Remember that you do not have all the answers. Your job is to keep the discussion going and encourage participation by everyone in the group.

Managing the Session

- Honor the time schedule. If a session is running longer than expected, get consensus from the group before continuing beyond the agreed-upon ending time.
- Consider involving group members in various aspects of the group session such as: playing the DVD, saying prayers, or reading the Scripture.
- Understand that the subject of forgiveness may strike raw nerves with some of the group members. Be alert for this, and do not press too hard if someone is showing signs of discomfort.
- Note that the session guides sometimes call for breaking into smaller teams. This gives everyone a chance to speak and participate fully. Mix up the teams; don't let the same people pair up on every activity.
- Confidentiality is essential because many activities call for personal sharing,. Group members should never pass along stories that have been shared in the group. Remind the group members at each session: confidentiality is crucial to the success of this study.
- You are the group leader. Prepare yourself with prayer as you begin your study of each chapter, as you ponder the learning activities in the leader guide, and as you prepare to lead. Then pray for each group member by name before each session. The Holy Spirit will lead and guide you.

1. More Than a Piece of Paper

Getting Started

Session Goals

As a result of conversations and activities connected with this session, group members should begin to:

- reflect on their own marriage or other significant relationship recalling the initial attraction, the growth of that attraction, and decisions about the future;
- identify and compare some realities of marriage with portraits of marriage painted by the popular culture;
- consider the involvement and participation of God in the marriage relationship;
- recognize marriage as a covenant not only with the spouse but with God;
- be able to define and illustrate the several classic Greek words that refer to love;
- honestly and forthrightly identify some dimensions of their own relationships, especially those dimensions that may need emphasis, clarity, or support.

Opening Prayer

When thinking of marriage, many people think first of the wedding. Endless hours of planning and preparation go into getting ready for the big day, and one of the major elements considered is what the bride and groom will wear. How many wedding dresses will the bride try on? Will the groom decide to wear a business suit, tuxedo, or something else? But the apostle Paul describes exactly what both parties ought to wear at the wedding and for every day of marriage beyond the big day.

Therefore, tell the group members that as the opening prayer for this session, you are going to read aloud Colossians 3:12-17. Pause after each phrase so that group members can reflect on the phrase, how it relates to their own relationship, and what might be needed to exemplify that phrase more completely in keeping with God's plan for marriage.

Conclude by inviting the group to join with you in the Lord's Prayer, reflecting as you do so on the phrase "Your will be done, on earth as it is in Heaven."

Biblical Foundation

Then the LORD God said, "It is not good that the man should be alone; I will make him a helper as his partner. . . ." So the LORD God caused a deep sleep to fall on the man, and he slept; then he took one of his ribs and closed up the place with flesh. And the rib that the LORD God had taken from the man he made into a woman and brought her to the man. Then the man said, "This at last is bone of my bones and flesh of my flesh; this one shall be called Woman, for out of Man this one was taken."

Genesis 2:18, 21-24

Opening Activity

Hamilton is forthright as he describes his initial attraction to the woman who was to become his wife, and he is equally honest as he tells us about the first days and weeks of his marriage.

Divide the group into teams of three, putting husbands and wives on different teams. Ask each team member to discuss the initial attraction to the person who became his or her spouse: some of the difficulties in moving from "love at first sight" to a more mature and substantial marriage, and some ways the marriage relationship has changed over the years. (Note: This is not a time for pseudo-therapy; it should be a joyful time of sharing, laughter, and memories.)

After each person in the team has had time to share, ask the teams of three to join another team of three and share highlights of their conversations. Do the team members sense any common themes in these descriptions? What are some of those common themes?

Reassemble as a large group then pose this question: based on our conversations, what are some things we can say about falling in love, deciding to marry, and maintaining a marriage?

Learning Together

Video Study and Discussion

Show the first video. Before doing so you might want to introduce Adam Hamilton, the book author and video presenter. Information about him can be found on the package.

In the first video, Hamilton uses three key words in describing how spouses ought to relate to one another. Ask the group to recall the words (*helper*, *partner*, and *companion*). Write these on the board as group members name them.

Divide the group into smaller teams, and ask them to discuss these questions:
- how are the three words alike;
- how are they different;
- can a spouse be all three things at the same time;
- can a spouse be only one or two of these things and still experience a happy and successful marriage?

Give reasons and examples.

Ask team members to describe times when they have experienced their spouses being each one of the key words. How do these roles change as situations change? Give some examples. Invite single members of the teams to describe how they have observed spouses taking each of these roles in their families of origin or in friends' marriages.

Back in the large group, have the teams share a few of their observations; then ask them to ponder this question: in your opinion which of the three roles is easiest to fulfill in a relationship? Why? Which is most difficult? Why?

Book Study and Discussion

In his book, Adam Hamilton makes a statement that some people might find surprising: "One of the most important things I can tell you about love, marriage, and sexual intimacy is that it's hard work." Hamilton could have put an exclamation point after that statement! Invite group members to turn to a neighbor, preferably not a spouse, and discuss Hamilton's statement. Do you think love, marriage, and sexual intimacy are "hard work"? Hard work for whom? Why? Is it true for everyone? Give reasons for your answers, and then turn to another discussion pair—again, preferably not including a spouse—and share responses, insights, and ideas.

Reassemble as a large group and ask some of the pairs and fours to share a few responses and reactions. Do all of them agree that love, marriage, and sexual intimacy are hard work? Why or why not?

Hamilton uses an apt phrase in the book and video: "the meaning and mission of marriage." What are some of the group's thoughts about the *meaning* of marriage? What about the *mission* of marriage? Working as a large group, spend a few moments writing a mission statement for marriage. Hint to the group leader: Do not spend too long on this; jot down some initial ideas, but be ready to edit, add to, delete, and polish this statement throughout the six sessions of this study.

Hamilton provides some fascinating data regarding the changing face of marriage. While these data are true and accurate, statistical data tend to be a bit lifeless. Divide the group into teams of six and ask each team to discuss some of the changes they have seen in marriage during their lifetimes. Encourage team members to think broadly: How has the institution of marriage changed because of such realities as economic issues, longer life spans, increased mobility, and images of marriage in motion pictures and television?

After the discussions call the large group back together to list some of the external forces that have changed the face of marriage over, say, the last thirty to fifty years. Would the group members' grandparents or great-grandparents recognize marriage today as being similar to what they experienced two or three generations ago? Give reasons and illustrations for your responses.

One of the changing realities of marriage in our time is the large number of couples who are living together without being formally married. Invite three members of the large group who enjoy acting to role-play some of the illustrations Hamilton suggests. One actor could be a pastor, and the other two could be a couple saying, in essence, "Why do we need a piece of paper to love and to be committed to each other?" Play out this conversation. Then choose different actors and change the scenario to a couple trying to convince their parents, using the same argument. Finally, play out the same scenario with the couple talking to one of their parents who is divorced. After the role-plays are completed, ask for feedback from the group. (Critique the situations, not the actors!)

Conclude this part of the discussion by asking the large group to imagine some ways that marriage may change in the next thirty to fifty years. List and discuss these ideas. Hint: Don't be afraid to name the elephant in the room: same-sex marriage. Will this trend continue? If so, how might it affect marriage as we know it today? Having acknowledged the elephant, however, don't let it derail discussion of the larger issue.

In the large group, discuss this question: If marriage is more than a piece of paper (that is, a legal contract called a *marriage license* that is issued by a government agency), in what way is it "more"? How can contemporary Christians who live in a confusing world remember and live out our belief that "more" is grounded in the presence and the intent of God? How do the Creation stories in the first two chapters of Genesis help illuminate what marriage is and what it ought to be?

In the chapter Hamilton states that marriage is a calling from God. While few Christians would argue with this statement, the crucial question becomes: How do we care for, bless, and serve one another in marriage?" In teams of three, ponder these questions:
- How do we learn to care for another in marriage?
- Are the needs of the other the same as our needs?
- How do we bless each other in the marriage relationship?
- What does this blessing involve in absolute and practical terms?
- What does it mean to serve one another in marriage?

Ask team members to describe and give examples of ways they have been blessed or felt served in their marriage. Point out that these actions are not to be taken lightly. Caring for one another, blessing one another, and serving one another must become a way of life for both partners in order for a marriage to last.

Back in the large group, hear quick reports from some of the teams of three, then discuss Hamilton's understanding of the Hebrew word *ezer*, the concept of the stronger coming to the aid of the weaker. ("The idea is not that a stronger person is brought in to serve the weaker, but that two people bring their mutual strengths to the relationship in order to bless one another.") What do you think of this concept? Give illustrations and examples of your answers.

In the large group, discuss two of the Greek words mentioned in the book that are translated as "love"—*eros* and *agape*. Which of these words is present in a strong marriage? (Hint: It's a trick question.) That's right. Ideally both kinds of love are present and active in a strong marriage.

How can we make sure our marriages contain both kinds of love—that we are truly caring for one another, blessing one another, and serving one another in a genuine and God-directed way? One eighteenth-century theologian spoke of "going on to perfection."[1] Are our marriages going on to perfection? How can we know? If they are not, how can we change their trajectory?

Bible Study and Discussion

Adam Hamilton uses the second Creation story, Genesis 2:18, 21-24, as the biblical background for this session. Invite group members to read this passage aloud, using whatever translations they have. Pose the following questions for discussion in groups of four, then in the large group:

What do you think this passage says about the equality of male and female in the marriage relationship?

How has this passage been used—or misused—over the centuries by those who would claim the dominance of one gender over another?

What fundamental ideas about the relationship of women and men do you think God was proclaiming in this Creation story?

How do the Creation stories in Genesis—the creation of woman and man—find expression and fulfillment in Paul's words for the Colossians that were considered as this session opened?

Wrapping Up

Remind group members that this study is just beginning and that the answers to some of the questions raised by Hamilton and by your discussions may take a lifetime to answer. Encourage group members to jot down questions that occur to them before your next session, and challenge them to put into practice in their own relationships at least one insight gained from the video, the book, the Bible, or the group discussion. Remind them that this study is not intended as therapy for a troubled marriage; it is an opportunity for all of us to consider God's plan for love and marriage, and for those of us who are already married to discover even more joy and fulfillment in our relationship.

Closing Prayer

Lord, guide us as we explore your plan for love and marriage. Help us to bless everyone in our lives, but especially our spouses. Lead us to discover together the meaning and mission of marriage. In Jesus' name. Amen.

2. WHAT SHE WANTS, WHAT HE WANTS

Getting Started

Session Goals

As a result of conversations, discussions, and the exchange of ideas during this session, group members should:

- continue to sharpen their understanding of the meaning and mission of marriage;
- reflect on those factors or characteristics that make them feel wanted, loved, and appreciated;
- reflect on those factors or characteristics that they think make their partners or potential partners feel wanted, loved, and appreciated;
- begin to come to some understanding of the languages of love and the nuances connected with the languages of love;
- grasp the concepts of "love tanks" and "love banks," reflecting on these and other metaphors for keeping a marriage vitally alive;

- begin to develop their own ways of caring for and blessing one another in the marriage relationship or a potential marriage relationship;
- honestly reflect on their own propensities to care for and bless their spouses or potential spouses in ways that the spouses need to be blessed.

Opening Prayer

Invite group members to write a prayer for marriage. Couples should work together on a prayer for their own marriage; singles can write a marriage prayer by themselves or with someone else. It's important for group members to follow through with this activity because they will continue to use the prayers and perhaps modify them as the study continues.

Ask one or two group members to share their prayers; then you or another group member might lead a time of prayer, focusing on enriching the already solid marriages and potential marriages within the group. Close with the Lord's Prayer.

Biblical Foundation

If then there is any encouragement in Christ, any consolation from love, any sharing in the Spirit, any compassion and sympathy, make my joy complete: be of the same mind, having the same love, being in full accord and of one mind. Do nothing from selfish ambition or conceit, but in humility regard others as better than yourselves. Let each of you look not to your own interests, but to the interests of others. Let the same mind be in you that was in Christ Jesus.

Philippians 2:1-5

Opening Activity

Divide the group into five teams; as always, try to separate husbands and wives as much as possible. Strive to make each team a balance of women and men. Assign each team one of the characteristics that are often sought by women and men in a marriage partner:

- honest/trustworthy,
- good communicator,
- strong faith,
- fun/humorous,
- emotionally stable.

Ask each team to discuss the assigned characteristic in some detail, indicating when and how one can know that the characteristic is present or absent. Remind the teams that they need to define their characteristic before they can begin to discuss it. What does it mean to be emotionally stable? How does a strong faith manifest itself in a relationship? What does it mean to be fun or humorous? Is it always cracking jokes, or is it something more than that; if so, what? What is involved in being a good communicator—for example, what part does listening play, and is communication always verbal? How can you tell if a person is honest?

Allow time for the teams to work on their characteristics, and then ask for a brief report from each team. As a team reports, jot down notes and insights from the team. Encourage the group members to quiz the reporting team, raising questions or contributing comments about the characteristic under discussion.

Then ask each member of the group to jot down the five characteristics she or he sought or would most seek in a marriage partner. Do not limit group members to this list of five characteristics. Ask group members to keep their lists for consideration later in the session.

Learning Together

Video Study and Discussion

Show the second video. Ask group members to jot down at least one new insight from the video. Remind them that insights can include questions and disagreements.

Consider one of Hamilton's opening statements in the video. He asserts that a marriage is a covenant between wife, husband, and God. Guide the group in exploring the concept of covenant. Can a covenant have three sides, between two human beings and God? What is the purpose of any covenant? Of the marriage covenant? In what ways can the marriage covenant provide a mutual blessing for each partner, including God?

Discuss Hamilton's observation that by helping each other selflessly, we are mirroring Christ's love for us. Ask group members to ponder what they do for others even though they may not wish to do so. In a marriage, what are some effects of this kind of selfless act?

Book Study and Discussion

For this part of the discussion, ask group members to take pencil and paper and to paraphrase—put into their own words—the saying mentioned in the chapter: "It is more important to *be* the right person than to find the right person."[2] Ask several group members to read their paraphrases, then pose the following questions for discussion by the whole group: What does the statement mean? Do you agree with it? Why or why not? More importantly, how can we know if we are being the right person?

Consider several points made by Adam Hamilton in the chapter. He suggests that we seek to discover what our spouses want. Invite group members to form pairs (no spouses) to respond to these questions: How can we know what our spouses or potential spouses want in the marriage relationship? Should we ask our spouses? How do we go about doing that? Do our spouses always know what they want, and can they articulate these wants in ways to which we can respond? Give some illustrations or examples for your answers. Hear brief reports from some of the pairs. Do most pairs agree on answers to these questions? If not, entertain comments or opposing views for a few moments.

Hamilton describes and discusses three metaphors for maintaining and strengthening a marriage relationship. Ask group members to identify these, and jot them down on the board (love languages, love tanks, love banks).

Ask group members to form teams of three to five people each and briefly consider these questions: How are the three metaphors alike, and how are they different? For example, is an "empty fuel tank" the same as an "empty bank account"? Once a fuel tank is empty or a bank account is overdrawn, can it ever be refilled? How? Is a refilled bank account or a refilled fuel tank the same after refilling as it was before it became empty? Give reasons and examples for your answers.

Still working in the smaller teams, ponder these questions: Hamilton suggests five types of love language based on work by Gary Chapman.[3] Review the five love languages (words of affirmation, quality time, receiving gifts, acts of service, and physical touch). Try as a team to define each love language in more detail than Hamilton provided in the book. For example, what does quality time mean? What is the relationship, if any, between receiving gifts and acts of service? Once the team seems to have a good handle on the meaning of these love languages, entertain this question: What other love languages would you add to this list? Let each member of the team suggest at least one other love language, and let the team help in defining this love language.

Now, still working in the smaller teams, consider some of Hamilton's comments with regard to love languages. He writes: "a man's and a woman's primary love languages are hardly ever the same."[4] First, do team members accept this assertion? If they do, how can a couple communicate and meet one another's needs? If a couple discovers that their love languages are different, how can they proceed so that each is fulfilled and blessed in the relationship? Must the couple play "My turn, then your turn" or some other adaptation? Or must one partner surrender his or her needs for the benefit of the other? Always? Ever?

Conclude the team discussions by raising this question: What part does an understanding of love languages play in a situation in which the fuel tank or the bank account is running dangerously low? Can one partner recognize when the other's tank is running dry? What can the partner do about that situation? How can this partner bless the other, the one whose tank is nearly empty?

Reassemble as a large group. Do not hear detailed reports from each team—this would take too long—but ask teams for any insights, questions, or conclusions they reached about love languages, fuel tanks, and bank accounts.

As a large group, discuss the concept of "investing in a marriage." Must each partner make equal contributions to the investment? Are these contributions always of the same kind? Give reasons and illustrations for your answers. If a couple has made little or no investment in their marriage, is it ever too late? If it is not too late, what are some ways to begin investing in it? How and where might the couple start? Can one partner in the couple "save" the marriage by investing in it even though she or he suspects that the other partner is not likewise investing?

What part does faith play when investing in a marriage? How can a couple know if their faith is helping to build their marriage? What practices of faith are necessary within a marriage for faith to have a positive impact on that marriage? Is simply going to church together sufficient? Give reasons for your answers.

Bible Study and Discussion
Ask a good reader to read aloud Philippians 2:1-5, the biblical passage for this session. Since the passage is short and important, you might ask them to read it aloud a second time.

Though Paul may not be writing specifically about the marriage bond in this passage, many of his points relate to what we've discussed in this session.

But is his counsel truly applicable to a marriage? Can a wife and a husband be in full accord and of one mind? Do you believe that Paul means it literally, or in some other way? If in another way, what is that other way? Does Paul mean that a husband and a wife must agree on everything, always, or is Paul speaking of something much more serious than the everyday decisions wives and husbands are called upon to make?

Divide the group into smaller teams and ask them to discuss what Paul might be saying here as it relates to marriage. How can a husband and a wife always be of the same mind without one or the other dominating? Or is Paul speaking of something much greater, or much less, than absolute agreement on every issue?

Continue in the smaller teams to discuss this passage: "Let each of you look not to your own interests, but to the interests of others." To what extent should both partners in a relationship surrender their needs, concerns, and wants for the benefit of the other? Always? Ever? How can one partner do this without doing so grudgingly?

Finally, discuss the final sentence in this passage: "Let the same mind be in you that was in Christ Jesus." What was and is the mind of Christ? How can we begin to adopt the mind of Christ as our mind? (Hint: It is only by seeking the best for others that we discover the best for ourselves, in marriage or in other relationships.)

Challenge group members to memorize Philippians 2:1-5 as a way of consciously putting Paul's words into practice day by day.

Wrapping Up

Remind the group about one of Hamilton's earlier statements: that marriage is "hard work." This study won't provide all the answers for a successful and growing marriage, nor will it heal a broken marriage. But perhaps the discussions during these six sessions should help all to see that love and marriage are not easy; both require work, effort, and endless self-giving and self-sacrificing love. That is what we have learned from our Savior, Christ Jesus.

Closing Prayer

Invite group members to a time of silent prayer. As they are in silence, softly suggest ideas about which they might be in prayer:

Think of a time when your love tank was empty. What happened? How was it refilled? Who helped refill it for you? Offer a prayer of thanks for that person or persons.

Think of a time when you encountered someone whose love bank was overdrawn. How did you reach out to that person and, using the languages of love, help them learn to make deposits in that bank account? Offer a prayer of thanks that God led you to that person and gave you the tools you needed to restore hope to that person.

Invite group members to join hands and to pray together the Lord's Prayer. Before beginning, ask them to focus especially on the petition that God's will be done on earth just as it is in heaven. Point out that it is in and through relationships that God's will is most effectively done.

3. The Significance of Sexual Intimacy

Getting Started

Note to the leader: You have a crucial role to play in this session; for in it group members will be discussing ideas and concepts that are not frequently considered in a church setting. Your approach in leading the group is key. You must deal with this subject forthrightly, honestly, openly, and genuinely, while recognizing and emphasizing all along that sexuality is part of God's plan for creation; therefore, it is very good.

Expect some discomfort among group members. Don't probe too much around issues related to sexuality. Be especially sensitive to those in the group who are single but plan to marry someday, those who have never married, and those who have been married but are not now. Again, you must set the tone for these discussions.

You may have one or more people in your group who simply are not able to discuss sexuality. Do not force them to do so, but in every case make discussion groups large enough so that those who choose to remain silent for any reason may do so. Needless to say, this is not a session that should include jokes or double entendres, but you may discover that some very gentle humor at the beginning of the session may give all a feeling of comfort and security.

You may want to remind the group that absolute confidentiality is both a hallmark and a prerequisite of your discussions.

These paragraphs are not meant to intimidate you as group leader. If you continue a relaxed and supportive attitude in leading the group, it will help overcome some anxieties on the part of group members.

Session Goals

As a result of conversations and activities in this session, group members should begin to:

- joyfully recognize expressions of human sexuality in relationships as a divine gift from God;
- reflect on societal attitudes toward human sexuality, contrasting these with the biblical views of human sexuality;
- recognize and celebrate the "life span" of human sexuality—that is, how the expressions of sexuality in a relationship change over the years;
- affirm that each individual and each marriage relationship is unique and need not measure up to "standards" implied by data;
- recognize and affirm the relationship between a strong, active faith in God and a growing, continuing joy in the marriage relationship.

Opening Prayer

Almighty God, you have created us for an intimate relationship with you and with one another. Despite what the world around us proclaims, teaches, and practices, help us to celebrate all the gifts you have given us, including the gift of sexuality. May we use this gift that your will might be done on earth as it is in heaven. We offer this prayer in the name of Christ Jesus. Amen.

Biblical Foundation

The husband should give to his wife her conjugal rights, and likewise the wife to her husband. For the wife does not have authority over her own body, but the husband does; likewise the husband does not have authority over his own body, but the wife does. Do not deprive one another except perhaps by agreement for a set time, to devote yourselves to prayer, and then come together again, so that Satan may not tempt you because of your lack of self-control.

1 Corinthians 7:3-5

Opening Activity

Divide the group into smaller teams. (If there are fewer than ten in your group, work as one big team.) In these teams consider the following questions:

- Where and how did you get information about human sexuality?
- How much of the information that you first learned had to be discarded and replaced with more accurate information?
- What, if anything, did you learn about human sexuality in Sunday school or church as a child and as a young person?
- Was it accurate information?
- Was the information affirming of human sexuality as a gift from God, or was it a series of "don'ts"?
- If you learned nothing about human sexuality as a child or teen in Sunday school, why do you think that was the case?

Hear brief reports from some of the teams, then pose this question for discussion by the large group: Why has the church remained largely silent in helping children and teenagers affirm sexuality as a gift from God, a gift to be celebrated and used according to God's will?

Learning Together

Video Study and Discussion

Show the video; then, if possible, repeat the first few minutes of the video, in which Hamilton makes a strong statement about the church's silence on the subject of sexual intimacy. Ask group members if any of them learned about sexuality in church, Sunday school, or youth group, and if so, what did they learn? If they did not learn about sexuality in church, where did they learn about it, and what did they learn? If your group includes a variety of ages, you may want to note and discuss any significant differences between answers of the older members and answers of the younger members.

Later in the video, Hamilton says that we need to learn to dance. Ask: What do you think he means?

Hamilton discusses three characteristics of sexuality in marriage. Ask group members to identify these from the video. (It allows us to be co-creators with God; it binds couples together; and it is a way of knowing another person honestly and intimately.) Which characteristics do group members feel are the most important? Why?

Book Study and Discussion

Note to the leader: Adam Hamilton's book *Love to Stay* contains considerable data regarding sexual activity in the marriage relationship. If the question arises in the group, clarify that these data are not intended to be used as benchmarks or ideals. Group members should not measure themselves or their marriage relationship by these data. The data are not prescriptive, not standards, and not in any sense measures to be achieved. Each person and each couple is unique, and we celebrate that fact.

Adam Hamilton makes the point that discussing sexual intimacy is difficult, even between marriage partners. As a large group, discuss why this may be so. What are some of the reasons faithful Christians, friends, and marriage partners have trouble expressing themselves about sexual intimacy? Moreover, why is such conversation usually filled with jokes, innuendos, and other cover-ups?

Since we are "bombarded with sex," why is the topic of sexual intimacy so often feared and avoided? You might brainstorm a quick list of the ways we are bombarded with sex. Hamilton mentions television and movies; how else are we constantly confronted with sexuality? What is the message being sent? As an example, consider the use of sex in advertising. Ads often seem to be telling us that we will be sexually proficient or at least attractive to the opposite sex if only we use this or that product. What is the underlying message? How does that message jibe with the gospel of Jesus Christ?

Working as a large group, identify the "three big ideas" that come from Scripture regarding sexual intimacy. (In sexual intimacy we co-create with God, we are bound together, and we come to know each other intimately.) Post these three ideas in front of the group for them to consider. Then divide the group into three teams, one team to discuss each of these big ideas.

Here are some questions the first team might discuss as it considers sexual intimacy as a way of co-creating with God. You might jot these questions on the board for the team to follow.

- In the Creation story, what was the first thing God told human beings? (Hint: Check Genesis 1:28a.)
- What does it mean to be fruitful and multiply? Does it mean that everyone should have sexual relations? Does it imply that those who choose not to have children or can't have children are failing at this commandment? Give reasons for your answers.
- Some nations and religions encourage large families; other nations intentionally limit the size of families.

Is either of these policies in keeping with God's first instruction to human beings?

- Hamilton writes that the possibility of reproducing imbues the sexual act with holiness. In our day, has the advent of "morning after" pills, contraceptives, and legalized abortion drained some or all of the holiness from sexual intimacy? Give examples and illustrations for your answers.

Here are some questions the second team might discuss as they consider sexual intimacy as a way in which God binds us together. Again, you might jot these questions on the board for the team to follow.

- Hamilton writes that sexual intimacy binds our bodies together in a way that creates an emotional link, deepening our love and affection for one another. What does this understanding say about when and how sexual intimacy might be undertaken?
- Can a quick, momentary encounter be genuine? What criteria should be used to answer this question and judge the depth of commitment that results?
- What advantages do you see in the establishment of this emotional link? Are there disadvantages? Explain your answers.
- The term *soulmates* is sometimes used to describe a couple who seem perfect for each other. Do you believe there are soulmates? What does the term mean to you?

Here are some questions the third team might discuss as they consider sexual intimacy as a way in which, literally and metaphorically, we come to "know" each other. Once again, you might jot these questions down on the board for the team to follow.

- Can a couple be of one flesh, knowing one another completely, without literally being naked together?
- Note that the word *naked* has many connotations; in the Scriptures it often means vulnerable, exposed, nothing hidden. How can a couple understand and celebrate this total self-giving, this absolute vulnerability?
- Is this "knowing" complete and entire, or is it a consistently growing, emerging appreciation of the other and of the blessing in the relationship? Again, give reasons for your answer.

Hear brief reports from the three teams, and help the group compare the answers.

In the large group discuss this question: Because wife and husband are two unique individuals, Hamilton points out that their needs and desires are not identical at all times and in all ways. This difference may make it difficult to form a mutually satisfying intimate relationship. What is Hamilton's counsel for this? How do we bless one another in our sexual relationships when our needs and desires may be different at the moment or over time? What must one or the other sacrifice, and must the sacrifice always be made by the same person in the partnership? Is this giving up of one's own needs and desires for the sake of the other a way of blessing the other? How? How about accepting the sacrifice of the other for your own sake—is this accepting a way of blessing the other?

Bible Study and Discussion

Invite the group to form several smaller teams. Ask each team to paraphrase Paul's words in 1 Corinthians 7:3-4 and write down their paraphrase. (*Paraphrase* means to put a statement into one's own words.) Reassemble as a large group to share and discuss the paraphrases. Ask: How does Paul's statement—and the various paraphrases of it—relate to the idea of mutual blessing through sexual intimacy?

Wrapping Up

As leader, you may want to remind the group that this study is not a counseling opportunity or a group therapy time. If some group members seemed troubled by the discussion in this session, you might meet with them in private, pray with them, and refer them to your pastor.

Closing Prayer

Loving God, you created us as sexual beings, and for this we thank you and praise you. You never said that our way would be easy, but you have promised to be with us in each moment of our lives. Help us to be aware of your presence even in our moments of greatest intimacy, for these too are part of your great gift to us and for us. We pray in the name of the Christ. Amen.

4. Habits That Hurt, Habits That Heal

Getting Started

Session Goals

As a result of conversations and activities connected with this session, group members should begin to:

- recognize, acknowledge, and even celebrate the inevitability of disagreements and conflicts in the marriage relationship;
- affirm the power of words to both hurt and heal in the marriage relationship and beyond;
- recall and emphasize that the mission and meaning of marriage is mutual blessing, care, and love;
- understand and recognize the destructive power of abuse in the marriage relationship, whether the abuse is verbal, emotional, or physical;
- recognize the varieties of addiction that can and do destroy marriage;
- become aware of ways in which innocent pleasure-seeking can become an addiction that can destroy a marriage, a family, or a person;

- acknowledge and learn to avoid some beginning steps to adultery;
- recognize and affirm the strengths God provides to avoid these destructive habits—strengths that can be bolstered by worshiping and praying together.

Opening Prayer

Lord, you have given us the power of speech, and we have misused that power by using words to wound and to hurt. Forgive us as we recall in silence some moments when our words have hurt others needlessly.

Lord, we pray in silence that you would help us cleanse our words and purify our speech, such that they will glorify you and build up our sisters and brothers in Christ.

We offer this prayer in the name of the Word who became flesh so that we might have life and have it abundantly. Amen.

Biblical Foundation

Let no evil talk come out of your mouths, but only what is useful for building up, as there is need, so that your words may give grace to those who hear.

Ephesians 4:29

For this is the will of God, your sanctification: that you abstain from fornication [sexual immorality, author's translation]; that each one of you know how to control your own body in holiness and honor.

1 Thessalonians 4:3-4

Let your fountain be blessed,
and rejoice in the wife of your youth,
a lovely deer, a graceful doe....
may you be intoxicated always by her love.

Why should you be intoxicated, my son, by another woman....

Proverbs 5:18-20

Opening Activity

Ask group members to share times when they have said something to a spouse or companion and instantly wished they could take it back. How did they handle the situation? How did the spouse or companion handle it? How was peace and harmony restored? Discuss how, once a word is uttered, it cannot be returned.

Ask a group member to read James 3:1-12, then affirm that all of us use and misuse words, say things we'd like to take back, and sometimes speak before we think, especially in moments of anger or frustration. All of us need to affirm our humanness and accept God's forgiveness for our lapses in judgment.

You don't need to hear reports from each team, but if some team members want to raise insights or ideas, allow them to do so.

Learning Together

Video Study and Discussion

Show the video. Ask group members to name three serious issues described by Adam Hamilton that can "shipwreck" a marriage. Post these on the board, and tell group members they will deal with these issues later in the session, during the book study and discussion.

Now divide the group into smaller teams. Ask each team to consider the following questions: If you were asked for three additional causes for the shipwreck of a marriage, what might these three be? See if each team of three can come up with three more causes of disunity in marriage. If some team members want to describe illustrations or examples of these three additional causes, encourage them to do so. Hint: If some teams have trouble getting started, you might "prime the pump" with examples such as finances, in-laws, differing life goals, and conflicts over child rearing.

Reassemble as a large group and hear reports from each team. Jot down their responses on the board. Help the group to recognize that many, many different factors can indeed shipwreck a marriage.

Book Study and Discussion

Hamilton discusses in some detail three very serious threats to a marriage relationship. Invite group members to name these three threats (abuse, addiction, and adultery) and write them on the board. Then ask the group: What other serious threats to the marriage relationship would you add to this list? Based on your experience with friends and acquaintances, what other threats pose very serious problems for a married couple? (Note: Hamilton mentions several other threats to marriages including: finances, in-laws, differing expectations, and living arrangements.)

Now turn the attention of the group to the three big threats that Hamilton describes in some detail. Divide the large group into three teams, and assign one of the three threats to each team. Teams can begin their conversations with the questions given below, but they can also follow their own interests and concerns as they discuss these significant threats. Here are starter questions for each of the three threats; you might jot these on note cards and give copies to each team.

Group 1: Questions Dealing with the Threat of Abuse
- What constitutes abuse in the marriage relationship?
- Who determines or should determine what is abuse—the abuser, the abused, or outsiders? Give reasons and illustrations for your answer.
- What constitutes verbal abuse?
- When and how does normal kidding around become verbal abuse?
- How and in what ways may one partner in a marriage relationship verbally abuse the other without knowing it—or without the other knowing it? Think here of

comments that you have heard being made to friends, coworkers, and others.

- What is the effect of verbal abuse on the abused person?
- What is the effect on the abuser?
- What can you conclude about verbal abuse in the marriage relationship?
- How might physical abuse be experienced in the marriage relationship? Again, give illustrations and reasons for your answers.
- Do married people ever have the right to physically strike their partners? Explain your answer in some detail.

Now prepare a brief role-play in which partners in a marriage relationship experience verbal abuse. Is this verbal abuse always one way, or might both partners verbally abuse each other? Ask the team members to act out an example of verbal abuse; then let the rest of the team respond to the role-play. What can the team conclude about abusive relationships in marriage?

Group 2: Questions Dealing with Addiction

Hamilton describes in some detail the insidious nature of addiction. Review this section and discuss it in some detail.

- Why does what satisfied yesterday not satisfy today in the same way?
- Why is pornography considered to be such a serious addiction? (The common perception is that it does not hurt others the way drug or alcohol addiction hurts others because it is private—just involving the computer and the individual.)
- What are some ways in which addiction to any substance or activity interferes with the marriage relationship?
- Who or what is the addict putting first in priority—self, spouse, or addiction? Give reasons and illustrations for your answer.
- Now turn to a consideration of the addict. Who or what

determines when an individual is addicted to a substance or an activity (gambling, pornography)? For example, what is the difference between visiting a casino once on a cruise ship and making regular weekly bets with a "bookie"?

- Consider this: In substance addiction, certain substances are considered gateway substances—that is, they open the gates toward more serious substance addiction. Are there similar gateway activities that lead to pornography or gambling addictions? Illustrate.

Now let the whole team work at developing a brief role-play in which one partner in a marriage confronts the other partner about an addiction. (Perhaps it would be better here not to deal with a pornography addiction.) Let the confronter describe what the addiction is doing to the family; let the addict argue that he or she can stop at any time, making promises to do so. Act out this role-play for the team and consider any insights, questions, or comments the team members might have.

Group 3: Questions Dealing with Adultery
- Define adultery.
- Is adultery always and only a physical act?
- What else might adultery involve? Give some illustrations.

Hamilton describes the "slippery slope" toward adultery. Review this sequence of events as a team, adding ideas or insights as you do.

- How can a person facing that slippery slope put on the brakes?
- Must both persons agree to apply the brakes, or can one individual do it alone?
- If an individual puts on the brakes and calls an end to the relationship, what happens to the other person?

- What responsibility does the "braker" have to the "brakee"?
- Consider this: You experience a flirtation at the office, mutual attraction, and genuine enjoyment of another person's company. You decide, for whatever reason, that it must end. How do you end the relationship, and what responsibility, if any, do you have toward the other person?
- What does your answer say about the priority of the marriage relationship?
- Shift a bit. Suppose one partner in a marriage relationship has committed physical adultery and is grief-stricken because of it. Should he or she confess it to the spouse, or is it better to end it without confession and the hurt it will cause?
- If the person decides to confess, do you think the relationship between husband and wife can ever be the same? Give reasons for your answer.
- How can forgiveness and reconciliation take place? (Remember that forgiveness does not erase the past; forgiveness gives us back the future that we have forfeited by our sinfulness.)

Now plan a brief role-play for the whole group. In this role-play, try to include how church attendance and active Christian discipleship can strengthen a marriage relationship so that the temptation of adultery can be minimized.

In the large group, discuss the meaning of the chapter title: "Habits That Hurt, Habits That Heal." Most of the conversation has been around hurtful habits; spend a few moments discussing a list of habits that heal in the marriage relationship.

Bible Study and Discussion
Hamilton quotes the Old Testament Book of Proverbs and two of Paul's letters as the biblical background for this session. Divide into three teams, and assign each team one of the three passages shown in the biblical background above.

Instruct the teams to answer these questions about their passage: What is this passage of Scripture telling us to do? How do we do it? For example, can we always avoid evil talk? How? Can we always abstain from lust? How? In the Proverbs passage, what is meant by the word *intoxicated*? Hear a brief report from each team. Then pose this question for the large group: What do these passages lend to our understanding of the mission and the meaning of marriage?

Wrapping Up

This has been another difficult session dealing with some fundamental concerns that touch all families, married couples, and singles. The discussions and activities illustrate again and again Hamilton's contention that the marriage relationship is not always easy, that it requires hard work, that it demands our constant attention, and that it can and should be filled with blessings and joy.

Closing Prayer

This session has considered several difficult issues: abuse, addiction, and adultery. Perhaps some in your group have been silently asking, "Am I having that problem? Are we?" Since you can't know everything that's going on in the minds and hearts of the group members, simply invite them to a time of silent prayer; encourage them to lay their concerns before God's throne of grace; then challenge them to listen in silence for God's word for them today.

Close by reciting the Lord's Prayer, as always giving special attention to the petition, "Your will be done, on earth as it is in heaven."

5. Clothe, Bear With, Forgive

Getting Started

Session Goals

As a result of conversations and activities connected with this session, group members should begin to:

- identify in themselves and others characteristics that could cause friction in a marriage relationship;
- acknowledge their propensities to irritate others by small and seemingly insignificant habits and behaviors;
- discover ways to acknowledge one's own faults and express in loving ways those things that cause irritation in the marriage relationship;
- evaluate the concept of an Annual Marriage Performance Review and consider using this technique either formally or informally;
- explore in some detail the concept of forgiveness including but not limited to: the apology, the statement of regret, the request for forgiveness, and forgiveness.

Opening Prayer

Read aloud Psalm 150 as a prayer, or you could "line out" the psalm—that is, you read a line aloud and the group repeats the line back to you. If you line out the psalm, use genuine expression and ask the group members to echo that expression—hear the cymbals clashing and the trumpets blaring the praise of God! Close with a time of silent prayers of thanksgiving and praise.

Biblical Foundation

As God's chosen ones, holy and beloved, clothe yourselves with compassion, kindness, humility, meekness, and patience. Bear with one another and, if anyone has a complaint against another, forgive each other; just as the Lord has forgiven you, so you also must forgive.

Colossians 3:12-13

Opening Activity

Ask the married group members to make two lists: one of five things about themselves that frustrate or annoy their partner and then another of five things that they find annoying about their partner. Ask single group members to make a list of five things about themselves that they imagine would annoy a marriage partner and then another list of five things that they would find annoying in a partner. Assure group members that they won't need to share their lists with anyone if they don't want to.

After the lists are complete, ask: Did anything on your lists surprise you? What was it, and why? (Group members can answer silently or share their answers aloud.) Why do you think some of the things you listed might annoy a spouse? What might you do about it? What might you say or do to help a spouse recognize this characteristic? What are some differences between having an annoying characteristic and simply being who one is that way—that is, are there some characteristics that can't or won't change?

Learning Together

Video Study and Discussion
Show the video, then ask group members to cite new ideas they have gained from it.

One of the classic prayers of the Christian faith was penned by twentieth-century theologian Reinhold Niebuhr. In it, Neibuhr asks to accept what he cannot change, change what he can, and learn to know the difference.

Divide into smaller teams and ask each team to discuss these questions: How does this prayer relate to my marriage relationship? How does it relate to my acceptance of all (all?) that my partner is, and how does it relate to my partner's acceptance of all that I am? Is it enough to say, "That's just who I am!" or are some changes reasonable to ask for?

Niebuhr's prayer ends with a petition for wisdom to know the difference. Where and how can we gain that wisdom in today's world, bombarded as we are by cultural traditions and stereotypes of marriage and of wives and husbands? What part do our Christian faith and our participation in the ministries of a congregation help us to gain that wisdom?

Hear reports from several of the teams, then invite group members to jot down—for their eyes only!—at least three characteristics of their spouse that they will accept and at least three of their own characteristics that they will try to change for the sake of the partner. Invite group members to keep these notes in pocket our purse and refer to them often during the coming week.

Book Study and Discussion
Hamilton lists some "turnoffs," for both men and women. Find those lists in the book, and ask group members to study them for a moment. Ask: How do you account for the similarities and differences on these lists?

Now divide the group into smaller teams, and ask each team to examine the two lists in some detail and to consider these questions: What do closed-mindedness, judgmentalism, moodiness, arrogance, and bragging have in common? Let the teams pursue this question for a few moments, then ask for a response from each team. You might post their responses on the board. Discuss what we can learn from the lists regarding underlying causes and possible solutions.

Ask the large group: What subtle and indirect messages do we communicate to our partners or potential partners by some of the annoying habits we cling to? What might husbands and wives do about these subtle messages? Might a husband or wife be overly sensitive to these subtle messages? Or not sensitive enough?

In the large group, discuss the concept of an Annual Marriage Performance Review, as described by Hamilton in the chapter. What was their reaction when they first read about it? In your group, do responses to the concept differ depending on whether group members have experienced a performance review in a job? Do they think an Annual Marriage Performance Review would work in their marriage or relationship? Why or why not? Could both partners in a marriage do this genuinely and impartially? If so, how? If not, why not? Give reasons for your answers. Would one or more couples in the group be willing to try a performance review before the next session and report back on how it went and what insights wife and husband gained from this tool?

Break into smaller teams and ask each team to write a one-sentence definition of forgiveness. Next, ask the teams to describe in one sentence what forgiveness does for the forgiver and in one sentence what forgiveness does for the forgiven. Finally, ask this question for consideration in the teams: Does forgiveness look to the past, to the present, to the future, or to all three? Give reasons and examples for your answers. Come back into the large group to share and compare answers.

Return to the smaller teams and ask them to ponder these questions: The Lord's Prayer includes the line "Forgive us our trespasses as we forgive those who trespass against us." A key word in this petition is the little word *as*. What does *as* mean in this context? What else can that simple yet key word mean, and how else can those additional meanings enrich our understanding of forgiveness? Hear brief reports from the teams, focusing especially on unusual and thought-provoking meanings of the forgiveness petition within the Lord's Prayer.

Return to the teams and consider this subject: When one asks for forgiveness, one is apt to hear one of several clichés. These clichés include, "Forget it; I have" or "It never happened; it's over." Ask the team members to recall other clichés. Then ask them to evaluate the clichés. Are these honest responses? Do these kinds of responses reestablish a relationship that has been damaged? Why or why not? If not, what other reactions might work better?

Now move to the concept of sequence in the act of forgiveness. When did Jesus forgive? Recall New Testament stories of Jesus forgiving. When did this forgiveness take place? The nineteenth-century Danish theologian Søren Kierkegaard wrote that the only true forgiveness is the forgiveness that is extended even before the offender has realized his or her offense. Is this possible in the marriage relationship? Why or why not? Ask team members to recall times when they have been forgiven without first asking for forgiveness. What effect does it have on a relationship? Consider the opposite: If one must ask for forgiveness, what power or authority does this request place in the hands of the person who is asked? Does this kind of power and authority belong in the marriage relationship? Why or why not?

Bible Study and Discussion

Read aloud Colossians 3:12-13 at least twice. Then in the large group, discuss verse 13*b*. How has the Lord forgiven us? What does that fact say about the way we ought to forgive one another? Now consider verse 12. What does it suggest about the common custom of asking for forgiveness before forgiveness is granted? Recall the power and authority discussion from earlier in the session. What new ideas has Paul introduced into the discussion?

Wrapping Up

Hamilton's comment about forgiveness and the re-establishment of relationships is one of the keys to this chapter. While forgiveness in the marriage relationship is crucial, so too is the concept of forgiveness in all relationships. Invite group members to reflect on and pray about the role, experience, and place of forgiveness in their relationships.

Closing Prayer

Invite the group members to a time of silence. Then raise these questions for silent reflection within the group:

Who do I need to forgive? Why haven't I done so?

Whose forgiveness do I need to seek? Why haven't I done so?

What characteristics of God's forgiving me must I put into all my relationships?

Close with the Lord's Prayer.

6. A LOVE THAT LASTS

Getting Started

Session Goals

As a result of conversations and activities connected with this session, group members should begin to:

- recognize and affirm the various seasons of marriage;
- develop an appreciation for each season, with its blessings and trials
- understand the types of interactions that enrich the marriage relationship at each season of marriage;
- affirm and practice statements of appreciation and thankfulness as one of many ways to keep the marriage relationship strong;
- recognize and build upon the role of a shared Christian faith throughout the marriage relationship, and
- understand and implement more fully the meaning and mission of marriage.

Opening Prayer

Almighty God, who created us for yourself and for one another, and who placed us in relationship one with another: We ask you to bless our marriage relationship and other relationships, now and in the future, as they pass through several different phases and seasons. Give us joy in our relationships; give us peace, fulfillment, and a constant sense of your presence in every moment so that we might indeed bless one another as we are blessed by you. We pray in the name of Christ Jesus our Lord. Amen.

Biblical Foundation

As God's chosen ones, holy and beloved, clothe yourselves with compassion, kindness, humility, meekness, and patience. Bear with one another and, if anyone has a complaint against another, forgive each other; just as the Lord has forgiven you, so you also must forgive. Above all, clothe yourselves with love, which binds everything together in perfect harmony. And let the peace of Christ rule in your hearts, to which indeed you were called in the one body. And be thankful.

Colossians 3:12-15

Opening Activity

Provide group members with a pencil and a sheet of paper, which they should turn horizontally. Tell them they are going to create a chart—for personal use only and not to be shared—showing varying satisfaction levels during their marriage or other relationship.

Along the left edge of the paper, they should write the following words: in the upper-left corner the word *great*, in the lower-left corner the words "*not very good*," and in the middle of the left edge the words *so-so*. Along the top edge they should write these words: on the left side, the word *beginning*; and on the right side, the word *now*.

Ask the group to think about the seasons of their relationship and how their satisfaction levels varied. They should draw a line left to right, up and down, to indicate how satisfied they were at various points in the relationship. This may take some time and thought. One good way to start is by having them identify events in the relationship that moved their satisfaction line up or down. Encourage them to erase and correct the line as they work—that's why they have a pencil and not a pen.

Those in the group who are unmarried may want to fill out the chart by anticipating their satisfaction levels in a potential marriage over the years. If some in the group have been married more than once, let them choose which marriage they want to chart—or chart both, using a different line for each marriage.

Caution the group members that running a straight line across the top is not being completely honest. As Hamilton points out, every marriage has its up and downs.

Assure the group members that these charts are for their eyes only, but ask them to keep the charts to refer to throughout the rest of the session.

When they finish their charts, discuss these questions briefly: Was charting satisfaction and fulfillment easy or difficult for you? Why do you think that is so? Did you discover anything about your relationship that you had not recognized before? Did the events that caused changes in the direction of your line coincide with some of the events that Hamilton cites as causing changes in a marriage?

Learning Together

Video Study and Discussion

Before showing this video, ask the participants in the group to call out briefly what they have learned from the videos – not the study book, but from the videos. You might list these on the chalkboard or newsprint.

Now show this final video. Ask for quick initial reactions from the whole group.

Divide once again into teams of five and consider these questions: Hamilton uses two very interesting metaphors this video: dance and harmony. Talk for a few moments in the teams of five about what each of these means. What is the significance of using musical metaphors for talking about human relationships, especially between wife and husband? If teams seem to have trouble getting started with this, remind them that a dance always involves two persons and that the dance is only complete and beautiful if both move in their individual appropriate ways. Similarly, help team members recognize that harmony is not two notes that sound exactly the same, but two notes of different tone that, sounded together, make music.

Hear brief reports from some of the teams, then pose this question for discussion by the whole group: How can and does an active faith in God, a faith that is thankful, truly bless any human relationship? In a sense, God is the completion of the musical chord, the final resolution that makes the hymn complete.

Book Study and Discussion

Hamilton focuses first on two key terms: *perseverance* and *commitment*. Divide the group into smaller teams, and ask the teams to write a one-sentence definition of each word as it applies to the marriage relationship. Ask the teams also to cite an illustration or example of each word.

Invite the teams to share their definitions and illustrations, then pose this question for discussion by the whole group: Why are perseverance and commitment necessary in the marriage relationship? Commitment is a key here: commitment to what or to whom? Is the commitment to the marriage partner or to the marriage relationship or to something else?

Hamilton asserts that the marriage relationship isn't always easy—that marriages face hard times, frustrations, and occasional cooling of the love that brought wife and husband together. Return to the smaller teams and discuss Hamilton's assertion. If any team members would be willing to share, let them briefly describe to their teammates some of the hard times and frustrations in their relationships. Consider: Were the hard times and frustrations brought about from within the relationship or from external forces? If external forces played a part, what are some strategies for maintaining a healthy relationship in the face of external pressures? What is the role of honest and open communication at such times? What are the implications for communication during all phases of a relationship?

In the smaller teams, plan a brief role-play about how to deal with internal and external forces on a relationship. Let the "husband" and "wife" (preferably not a real-life husband and wife) deal with some sample hard times and the frustrations. Here are possible situations to act out: (1) finances are tight, and the husband or wife makes a large purchase without consulting the spouse, (2) husband or wife wants to take a new job to help with family finances, working the night shift while the spouse works the day shift, (3) husband or wife's mother wants to move into the spare bedroom; she is healthy physically but facing the onset of dementia.; (4) husband or wife wants to go out with friends one night a week on a regular basis.

Let the teams present their role-plays in front of the large group. Following each role-play, get the group's reactions. How were perseverance and commitment demonstrated or not demonstrated? How was honest communication demonstrated or not demonstrated? How could the couples in these role-plays have resolved their difficult times more effectively?

Hamilton discusses two times of life that may put special pressure on the marriage relationship: the time when children are in the home and careers are developing, and the transition into the empty nest and retirement.

Discuss briefly as a group some reasons why children in the home and the pressure for career advancement make that particular season in the marriage relationship difficult. If your group includes some couples who have weathered this difficult period, ask them to share some things they did to keep their marriages strong during that time. Keep the discussion light and informative. How did the couples share household chores? How did they deal with outside job pressures? How did they resolve differences? How did they find or make time for each other in the midst of the other pressures? And, very significantly, what role did their Christian faith play in keeping their marriage relationship strong?

Does your group include empty-nesters or retired couples? Ask them to share their experiences, again keeping the discussion light but helpful. What adjustments were required because of the absence of children at home or the presence of both spouses? What strains, if any, were put on the relationship? What role did (or could) the church and the Christian faith play?

Encourage each group member to jot down a completion of the following sentence, for his or her eyes only: "As a result of what I've heard today, I will strive to _____ in my marriage relationship." The unmarried members of your group might complete this sentence: "As a result of what I've heard today, I want to be sure that I _____ when I marry."

To close, raise this question for discussion by the group: Why is saying "thank you" to a spouse sometimes difficult? How can we learn to express our gratitude to our spouse—and to God—more genuinely and consistently?

Bible Study and Discussion

Refer again to Colossians 3:12-15. Working in smaller teams, read the passage aloud—several times if necessary. Then list, one by one, Paul's directions for a fulfilled and blessed life together. Which of these directions are easy to follow? Which are more difficult? Why? What, according to Paul, is the correlation between how we treat our spouses or future spouses and how we treat ourselves?

Wrapping Up

This week it's time to wrap up not just the session but also the entire study. Ask the group what parts of the book, videos, and group sessions were the most meaningful to them. Why? Did they learn things that might make a difference in their marriages or their lives? If so, what were those things, and why were they important? How will group members apply those learnings?

Closing Prayer

Distribute paper and pencils. Ask group members to write a very personal prayer for their marriage or other relationship. The prayer will be for their eyes only and may include petitions for God's guidance through the rough seasons of the marriage relationship. Encourage group members to use the prayer daily for at least the next six weeks, then rewrite portions of the prayer as needed, and use the revised prayer for six more weeks.

Close the session, as you have so many others, with the group praying aloud together the Lord's Prayer.

Notes

1. John Wesley (1703–1791), the founder of Methodism, first preached about the idea of Christian perfection around 1725. This theory can be explored in his work "A Plain Account of Christian Perfection," found in *The Works of John Wesley* (1872 ed. by Thomas Jackson), vol. 11, pp. 366-446.

2. Adam Hamilton, *Love to Stay: Sex, Grace, and Commitment* (Nashville: Abingdon Press, 2013), 37.

3. Author, pastor, and relationship expert Dr. Gary Chapman first spelled out his theory of emotional love in his book *The Five Love Languages: The Secret to Love That Lasts*, published by Northfield Publishing in 1992.

4. Hamilton, *Love to Stay*, 39.

Made in the
USA
Columbia, SC